Penguins!

Text and Photography by Wayne Lynch

FIREFLY BOOKS

A FIREFLY BOOK

Published by Firefly Books Ltd. 1999

First Printing

Canadian Cataloguing in Publication Data

Lynch, Wayne
  Penguins!

Includes index.
ISBN 1-55209-421-9 (bound)
ISBN 1-55209-424-3 (pbk.)

1. Penguins—Juvenile literature. I. Title.

QL696.S473L945 1999   j598.47   C99-930380-5

Published in Canada in 1999 by
Firefly Books Ltd.
3680 Victoria Park Avenue
Willowdale, Ontario
M2H 3K1

Produced by
Bookmakers Press Inc.
12 Pine Street
Kingston, Ontario K7K 1W1
(613) 549-4347
tcread@sympatico.ca

Design by
Janice McLean

Color separations by
Quadratone Graphics
Toronto, Ontario

Printed and bound in Canada by
Kromar Printing
Winnipeg, Manitoba

Library of Congress Cataloging-in-Publication Data

Lynch, Wayne.
  Penguins! / text and photographs by Wayne Lynch. 1st ed.
[64] p. ;   col. ill. ;   cm.
Summary : Introduction to penguins, from birth to adulthood, their communities and daily lives, illustrated with full-color photos and lively text.
ISBN 1-55209-421-9 (hc.)
ISBN 1-55209-424-3 (pbk.)
1. Penguins—Juvenile literature. [1. Penguins.] I. Title.
598.47—dc21   AC   1999   CIP

Published in the United States in 1999 by
Firefly Books (U.S.) Inc.
P.O. Box 1338, Ellicott Station
Buffalo, New York
14205

The Publisher acknowledges the financial support of the Government of Canada through the Book Publishing Industry Development Program for its publishing activities.

For Aubrey, as always

Field biologists often work under difficult living conditions and are driven solely by their quest to understand the natural world and the fascinating wild creatures that live in it. In my research on penguins, I spent hundreds of wonderful hours reading the scholarly words of field biologists. These dedicated men and women helped me to understand the world of penguins, and I am indebted to them all.

This is my fifth book with the friendly, capable folks at Bookmakers Press. As before, it was an easy and pleasurable task to work with editor Tracy Read, her partner and copy editor Susan Dickinson and designer Janice McLean. We've got to stop enjoying ourselves in this business; people are starting to talk.

I would also like to acknowledge the help of my longtime friend Joe Van Os of Joseph Van Os Photo Safaris, who continues to hire me to lead trips to the remote haunts of penguins.

Finally, this is my twelfth book, and for the twelfth time, I would like to dedicate it to the most deserving person in my life—my wife of 25 years, Aubrey Lang. At the risk of repeating myself, she is the most interesting, stimulating, loving, compassionate, unselfish person I know. I love her dearly.

CONTENTS

When the tide goes out along the coastline of Antarctica, the water level may drop 6½ feet (2 m) or more, creating a large shelf of ice that is impossible for Adélie penguins to leap from or onto. The landlocked penguins have to sit tight and wait for the tide to rise again.

INTRODUCTION

I made my third trip to Antarctica in 1997. On my final day on the continent, I went ashore at a huge Adélie penguin colony, where 125,000 pairs of black-and-whites nested from the shoreline to the tops of every ridge. I wandered around the colony for nearly 12 hours; it was one of the best penguin-watching days I have ever had.

No matter where I looked in the colony, penguins were on the move: tobogganing over the glistening snow on their bulging bellies, porpoising through the silver water like star-studded dolphins and waddling up slopes of rock with their flippers bouncing. There were penguins screaming and fighting with their neighbors, while others offered gifts of precious pebbles to their mates. Still others warmed and fed their wobbly-necked young. I laughed again and again when the nesting birds carelessly squirted each other with blasts of sloppy pink guano.

My best experience, however, came at the end of the day. I sat on a shelf of ice along the shoreline and watched gangs of penguins leap out of the water like rockets—who says penguins can't fly? One of the soaring birds miscalculated its approach and landed squarely in my lap. With an indignant squawk, the startled penguin tumbled off and hurried away.

By the early 1990s, I had spent 10 years studying bears and had written three books about these impressive carnivores. On my first trip to Antarctica, many people assumed that I was going there to continue my study of bears. Of course, there are no bears in Antarctica or anywhere else that penguins live. I went to Antarctica simply to see how it compared with the Arctic, and unexpectedly, I fell in love. Penguin colonies were like nothing I had ever seen before—so much activity, so much noise, so many odors, so much life. Perhaps it was the penguins' unwary nature, their familiar upright stance or their comical waddle that won my heart. It didn't really matter why I found penguins interesting—I was hooked.

My search for penguins has taken me from the frozen edges of Antarctica and the wave-battered shorelines of New Zealand's Antipodes Islands to the sun-scorched beaches of the Galápagos Islands and the rugged coast of Chile's Atacama Desert. For me, penguins have become more than cute birds that waddle and bray; they are exciting creatures with lives as complicated as our own. In *Penguins!* I will share with you the exciting details of how these flightless seabirds thrive in their world. It is not only a wonderful story of scientific discovery but also a story filled with surprises and tantalizing secrets.

The rockhopper, one of the crested penguins, is a real loudmouth. One writer compared the noise at a rockhopper colony to that of "thousands of wheelbarrows, all badly in need of greasing, being pushed at full speed."

CHAPTER 1

WHAT IS A PENGUIN?

The first Europeans to see penguins were the sailors in wooden ships that creaked and pitched around the southern capes of Africa and South America about 500 years ago. The grizzled seafarers who weathered these storm-battered waters couldn't decide whether penguins were mammals, birds or fish, so they settled on "feathered fish." They were half right. Penguins are covered with feathers, but they are definitely birds, flightless seabirds. Today, there are 17 different kinds of these "feathered fish."

Penguins were not always flightless. Researchers now believe that penguins evolved from a group of flying seabirds called tubenoses, so called because their nostrils are located at the end of a tube on the top of their beaks. Today, the tubenoses include albatrosses and petrels, some of the greatest fliers in the world. According to scientists, the earliest penguins branched off from the tubenose group around 65 million years ago, about the same time the dinosaurs disappeared.

The Maori of New Zealand have an old legend about how the first penguin became flightless. Back in the distant past, a penguin named Tawaki and an albatross called Toroa argued continually about which of them was better at fishing and flying.

The constant bickering annoyed Tane-mahuta, the god of the forests and birds, and he took the two birds aside and gave each of them a special skill. To Toroa, he gave the longest wings of any seabird so that the albatross could soar on the ocean winds far from land in search of food. To Tawaki, he gave powerful flippers so that the penguin could fly beneath the ocean waves to catch all the fish it would ever need.

Paleontologists offer an even better explanation about how the penguin lost its wings. The earliest penguins were relatively small flying seabirds, no bigger than the present-day puffin. Like puffins, these penguins used their wings both to swim underwater and to fly in the air. Since water is much denser than air, no wing can work equally well in both places. The reasons for this are simple. In air, a bird's wings provide lift as well as forward motion, and they need a relatively large surface

The king penguin is the second largest of the 17 species of penguins alive today. An adult king can stand as tall as 37½ inches (95 cm) and weigh up to 35 pounds (16 kg).

area to accomplish this. In short, they function like sails. In water, on the other hand, most birds are neutrally buoyant, so they don't need their wings for lift, only for forward motion. The best underwater wings act like paddles and have a relatively small surface area. Early in their evolution, penguins gave up flying in favor of improved underwater swimming. Their wings became modified into small, stiff flippers that could propel them underwater faster and deeper than any other bird. The flightless penguins had arrived.

Once penguins no longer needed their wings for flight, they could get much bigger—and they did just that. Today, the largest penguin alive is the emperor, which stands over three feet tall (90 cm) and can weigh 88 pounds (40 kg) or more. Among the early penguins, nearly half were larger than the emperor is today, and some species were very much larger. The largest penguin ever discovered, *Anthropornis nordenskjoeldi*, has no common name, but if

I met one in a dark alley, I would call it "sir." The burly Anthropornis stood as much as 5 feet 7 inches tall (170 cm) and may have weighed nearly 300 pounds (135 kg).

For many millions of years, penguins were the main warm-blooded predators of fish, squid and krill in the southern oceans of the world. When the dinosaurs became extinct, many marine reptiles also disappeared, and penguins simply took their place. The reign of the penguin clan lasted for perhaps 15 to 20 million years, during which time there were as many as 40 different kinds of these flipper-powered predators roving the seas. Then, about 15 million years ago, the seals, sea lions and small toothed whales arrived on the scene, and everything changed. Suddenly, the penguins, especially the large species, were faced with some fast-swimming competition, and the penguins lost. When the sea spray settled, only the smaller penguins had survived. Those are the species we have with us today.

Courting black-browed albatrosses, **left**, caress each other with their beaks. These birds may not breed for the first time until they are 6 or 7 years old. Both the giant petrel, **right**, and the albatross belong to the group of seabirds called tubenoses, which includes some of the greatest fliers on Earth. Tubenoses are the closest living relatives of the flightless penguins.

Meet the Family

In 1914, author Murray Levick described a penguin in this way: "Imagine a little man, standing erect, provided with two broad paddles instead of arms, with a head small in comparison with the plump, stout body; imagine this creature with his back covered with a black coat …tapering behind to a pointed tail that drags on the ground, and adorned in front with a glossy white breastplate. Have this creature walk on his two feet, and give him at the same time a droll little waddle and a pert movement of the head; you have before you something irresistibly attractive and comical."

Levick was describing an Adélie penguin, the species commonly pictured in advertising and the one many people think of as the typical penguin. Today, however, most scientists recognize 17 different kinds of penguins, which are divided into six groups.

The largest group of penguins in the family includes the six crested species: royal, macaroni, rockhopper, erect-crested, fiordland and Snares. All of them have wispy yellow or orange head plumes and a feisty disposition to match their wild hairdos. The medium-sized crested penguins stand roughly two feet tall (60 cm) and weigh anywhere from 5 to 18 pounds (2-8 kg). One of the largest crested species, the macaroni penguin, is the most populous of all, boasting 11.8 million breeding pairs. In fact, nearly half of all the penguins in the world are macaronis.

The four banded penguins (magellanic, Humboldt, African and Galápagos species) compose a second group. They are sometimes called jackass penguins, because all of them bray like donkeys. When a whole colony of these loudmouths begins to holler, the racket can be deafening. All the banded penguins have either a single or a double black band across the upper chest and are small to medium in size, weighing between 4 and 14 pounds (2-6.5 kg). Among the banded penguins, the survival of two of them —the Galápagos and the Humboldt species—is currently threatened, and both penguins, which occur in the Pacific, have small, vulnerable breeding populations ranging between just 5,000 and 8,500 pairs.

A third group of penguins is the brush-tailed penguins, which includes the familiar tuxedo-clad Adélie, the chinstrap and the gentoo. The chinstrap, like the Adélie, is a plain black-and-white penguin with pudgy pink feet. The

The crest of the macaroni penguin, **top**, earned this bird its peculiar common name. In the 1700s, an unruly hairstyle was popular in England among rich young gentlemen, and followers of the fad were called "macaronis." The gentoo, **bottom**, is the largest of the trio of brush-tailed penguins. Until it is 3 or 4 weeks old, a gentoo chick is guarded continuously by one of its parents.

11

gentoo, by comparison, is the most colorful of the three, with a bright orange beak and a matching set of color-coordinated feet. Members of the brush-tailed trio are medium in size, weighing between 7 and 14 pounds (3-6.5 kg), and all have a longer-than-usual tail of stiff quills, from which the group derives its name.

The two largest penguins, the king and the emperor, make up a fourth group. Their size —an average 33 pounds (15 kg) in kings and 77 pounds (35 kg) in emperors—enables them to perform feats of endurance beyond the capabilities of the smaller species. Between them, the king and the emperor dive the deepest, withstand the coldest winter temperatures and travel the farthest on feeding trips of any of the penguin species.

The last two groups of penguins each contain a single species. In one group, there is the handsome yellow-eyed penguin; and in the other, the little, or fairy, penguin. The little penguin is the smallest member of the penguin family, weighing less than three pounds (1.5 kg) soaking wet. The yellow-eyed species, by comparison, is a real bruiser and can be six times heavier than the little penguin. Unfortunately, size is no guarantee of survival, and the yellow-eyed penguin, which lives in New Zealand, is the most endangered of all the penguin species. As few as 1,600 breeding pairs remain.

It is one thing to divide the penguin family into six compact groups and quite another to identify which bird is which. Body size is a good place to start, since each species generally falls into a single category: small, medium or large. Beyond that, plumage pattern is the main key to penguin identification. All 17 species have roughly the same body coloration: dark gray or black on the back, with a bright white chest and belly. This common color pattern has led naturalists to joke that there are really just two kinds of penguins: the black ones running away from you and the white ones coming toward you.

When a penguin is floating quietly on the surface of the water, only its head and neck are visible. Luckily, these parts of the bird carry many identifying characteristics: differences in the size and color of the bill; the presence or absence of a bright, conspicuous crest; and distinctive patterns of color on the head and neck. Penguins likely rely on the appearance of these body parts to identify each other. Human bird

The rare yellow-eyed penguin, **top**, frequently nests in forests among ferns and other greenery. It is the least sociable of all the penguins; in fact, if it can see its neighbors, it often abandons its nest for another site. The little penguin of New Zealand and Australia, **bottom**, is the runt of the family. It would take 30 little penguins to equal the weight of a single emperor, the largest penguin.

watchers use these same clues to distinguish the different species.

Worldwide, there are over 9,600 bird species. Obviously, the 17 species in the penguin family represent a very tiny proportion of these. Yet for such a small family of flightless birds, penguins have managed to occupy a greater range of latitudes and temperatures than almost any other avian family on Earth.

Penguin Places

When most people think of penguins, they think of Antarctica, icebergs and numbing cold. They think of tough birds beaten by blizzards,

King penguins and royal penguins loaf away the day on a beach on Macquarie Island, roughly halfway between the southern coast of Australia and the icy coast of Antarctica. This one small island is the only place in the world where royal penguins nest.

huddling over their nests on frigid sea ice or bare rock. Although two penguin species—the Adélie and the emperor—actually live like this, most penguins live where the conditions they face are much different.

Penguins evolved in the southern hemisphere, probably in the cool ocean waters between 50 and 55 degrees south latitude. Today, these same waters south of New Zealand are home to nine penguin species, a greater variety than exists anywhere else on Earth. But the early penguins had wanderlust, and they gradually paddled their way into other areas of the ocean north and south, until they finally ranged from the icy shores of Antarctica to the searing sands of the equator. Today, penguins live with koalas in southern Australia and parrots in New Zealand. In southern Africa, they make their homes alongside lions and hyenas, and in the Galápagos Islands, the local penguins share the shoreline with marine iguanas. Clearly, penguins are extremely adaptable birds.

Oceans cover more than three-quarters of the southern hemisphere, and you might expect an adaptable seabird such as the penguin to live wherever there is salt water. Not so. Penguins are not evenly distributed over the vast oceans of the hemisphere. Ocean areas differ greatly in the amount of plankton they produce. A number are particularly rich and have therefore attracted the greatest numbers of penguins. Predictably, penguins are at home where the fish are jumpin' and the livin' is easy. Wherever cold oxygen-charged water, rich in nutrients, mixes and wells to the surface, plankton multiplies as a result, and the fish, krill and penguins follow. Such areas occur along the southwestern coastlines of South America and Africa, where they are called the Humboldt and

Benguela currents, respectively. Three species of penguins are nourished by these fertile, cold coastal currents.

Rich upwellings also occur in the Antarctic Peninsula and along the coastlines of several dozen island clusters scattered around the entire perimeter of the continent. Islands such as South Georgia, the South Sandwiches, Kerguélens, Crozets and Macquarie are world-renowned for their huge penguin colonies.

Finally, the Antarctic Convergence is another rich ocean area where penguins concentrate. Here, the cold, dense waters of the Southern Ocean that surrounds Antarctica meet and dip beneath the warm, saltier waters of the southern Atlantic, Indian and Pacific oceans. The mixing of the different waters creates ideal conditions for the growth of plankton, and penguins profit as a result.

With so many penguins thriving in the cold waters of the southern hemisphere, why are there none in the northern hemisphere? A major barrier to penguins moving north is the warm waters of the Tropics, which are relatively poor in dissolved oxygen and nutrients. In such waters, penguins would have trouble finding enough food to fuel them on their long journey north. Thus thousands of miles separate most penguin populations in the south from the cold, rich northern waters of the Atlantic and Pacific. Penguins could live in the cold waters of the northern hemisphere if only they could get there.

During the 1930s, Norwegian whalers transported and released several dozen king penguins, chinstraps and macaronis off the northern coast of Norway. Some of the transplanted penguins lived for more than 10 years, but none ever bred, and all of them eventually disappeared.

Hot & Cold Penguins

The body temperature of an emperor penguin huddled in a winter blizzard in Antarctica at minus 40 degrees F (−40°C) is the same as that of a Humboldt penguin loafing on the coastline of the Atacama Desert in Chile at 108 degrees F (42°C). There is, however, one big difference. The emperor must conserve body heat to keep from freezing to death, and the Humboldt must shed body heat to avoid being cooked alive. The penguin family has evolved a fascinating series of adaptations to deal with such temperature extremes.

The royal penguin's sizable body makes it more resistant to cooling. One of the largest of the crested penguins, it can survive in the cold waters around the Antarctic Convergence.

A thick layer of feathers helps all birds stay warm. The penguin has carried this adaptation a step further. A penguin's body feathers are surprisingly small for the size of the bird. Most of the feathers are lance-shaped, with a stiff vein down the center and a small tuft of down at the base. Because of their design, the feathers overlap like roof tiles and are not easily ruffled in the strong winds that can rob a penguin of body heat. The tufts of down add further insulation by trapping a layer of warm air next to the bird's skin.

The penguin has two other aces up its flippers. First of all, a penguin's body is covered with feathers; the feathers on most other birds are arranged in tracts, with bare spaces in between. You can discover this for yourself by examining the pattern of small bumps on the skin of a roasted turkey or chicken. The bumps are feather follicles. Notice how they are clustered on the skin and how some areas of the skin have no follicles at all. The complete feather covering on a penguin provides better insulation than if the feathers were arranged in tracts. Finally, every square inch of a penguin's body has up to 80 feathers packed into it, three to four times more feathers than in any other group of seabirds.

It is not enough for some penguins simply to conserve body heat with a thick covering of feathers. They must also be protected against excessive heat loss from their beaks, flippers and legs. A comparison between the polar emperor penguin and its close relative the king, which lives in a warmer climate, will illustrate how some penguins beat the chill. Even though emperors are twice as heavy as king penguins, they have shorter beaks, shorter flippers and smaller feet. All these adaptations lessen the loss of body heat. Furthermore, the legs of an emperor penguin are covered with feathers—only its toes are bare—while both the legs and the toes of the king penguin are bare.

Flipper and beak adjustments can also occur in a single species of penguin that lives in a wide range of climates. For example, gentoo penguins nesting at 65 degrees south latitude on Pleneau Island, along the Antarctic Peninsula, have shorter beaks and flippers than gentoos nesting 900 miles (1,450 km) farther north, on the relatively warm Falkland Islands.

When they can't shorten their beaks any further, some penguins use another heat-saving

Reaching 77 degrees south latitude, the Adélie, **top**, nests farther south than any penguin species. The feathering at the base of its beak is an adaptation to cold. **Bottom**, the bare skin on the Humboldt penguin's face, on the other hand, helps the bird shed excess body heat as it nests in the hot sun along the coast of Chile's Atacama Desert.

15

device—feathers. This adaptation is best illustrated in the three closely related members of the brush-tailed penguin group. The gentoo penguin, which generally nests in the warmest conditions of the three, has no feathers insulating its beak. The chinstrap, which nests in colder climates, has feathers covering the inner third of its beak. The Adélie, which nests farther south than any penguin—77 degrees south latitude—has half its beak wrapped in fine feathers. Another way that penguins can conserve body heat is to tuck their beaks under a warm flipper when they are sleeping.

Everyone has heard about blubber, the fat that covers the bodies of seals and whales. It insulates the animals against the cold and also provides them with a handy energy reserve. Fat on the bodies of some penguins may be nearly an inch (2.5 cm) thick. You might think that these birds could also rely on their fat to insulate them against the cold waters in which they swim, but this is not the case. Scientists now believe that penguins use their fat mainly as an energy reserve and not as a heating blanket. In fact, when some of the large penguins, such as kings and emperors, dive, they *need* to lose body heat to stay underwater longer. I will talk more about this exciting new discovery later.

The final way in which penguins can stay warm is to huddle. Once they reach the age of a month or so, the chicks of many penguin species clump together when the weather gets bad to share body heat. However, the real test of huddling as a heat saver is seen in the adult emperor penguin. In this species, each male must incubate a single egg through the worst of the antarctic winter. In some large emperor colonies, several thousand adult males may huddle together, eight birds per square yard

(10/m²), to withstand the numbing cold and winds of a blizzard. The temperature inside the huddles may be 18 Fahrenheit degrees (10C°) warmer than the outside air, and this means energy savings for the huddlers. Emperors outside a huddle lose twice as much weight as those crammed into the crowd. Since an incubating male emperor may need to fast and stretch its fat reserves for up to three months, it needs to save as much energy as it can. Without these huddles, a male emperor could never fast this long, and it would have no choice but to abandon its egg and head back to sea.

Since penguins evolved in a cool oceanic environment, it's no surprise that they're well

Young rockhoppers, **top**, huddle together not only in cold weather but also in warm weather, to lessen the risk of attack from predators. All penguins are able to squeeze oil from a nipple-shaped gland at the base of the tail, **bottom**. The oil waterproofs their feathers, keeps their beaks from drying out and also protects them from bacteria.

adapted to keeping warm. But how do the well-insulated birds cool off? Every penguin builds up body heat when it is swimming, even in the coldest water, so all penguins need some way to get rid of excess heat. One way is to send blood to the flippers. The feathers on a penguin's flippers are small and scalelike and have very little insulation. Warm blood diverted to the flippers is therefore quickly cooled by the surrounding water or air. When a penguin first lands on shore, its flippers are often flushed pink with blood; the bird holds them out from its sides to allow the air to cool them.

The greatest adaptations to prevent over-heating are found in the banded penguins, the species that live in the warmest climates. As I mentioned earlier, a penguin loses body heat through its beak, but it can also lose heat through the skin on its face. The faces of all the cold-climate penguins are covered with feathers, but this is not so in the warm-weather species. In magellanic and African penguins, the birds have bare, featherless skin between their eyes and at the base of their beaks. In the Humboldt and Galápagos penguins, the bare area is larger and extends beneath the beak as well. When these birds build up too much body heat, they simply divert more blood to the skin of their faces to cool off. Humans do something very similar. After a long run, a jogger's face is as red as a beet.

For Adélie penguins in Antarctica, 39 degrees F (4°C) is a heat wave. To cool off, the birds pump blood to their flippers. Since the feathers on the underside of their flippers are small and thin, body heat can escape more easily.

CHAPTER 2

PENGUINS IN MOTION

Penguins spend most of their lives at sea. Some species may not even touch land for six or seven months at a stretch. Fiordland penguins, which belong to the crested group, may ride the swell off the coast of New Zealand for such long periods that barnacles begin to grow on their tail feathers. Clearly, penguins are most at home in the water, and if there is one thing they do well, swimming is it.

A penguin may never win a beauty contest for its curves and hourglass figure, but it has the perfect torpedo shape to slice through the water. When a penguin is swimming underwater, its head is tucked snugly between its shoulders and its feet trail behind, making the bird as streamlined as possible. The fastest penguin swimmers are the large species—the kings and the emperors. A flipper-powered emperor can torpedo through the water at up to nine miles per hour (14.5 km/h), nearly twice as fast as an Olympic swimmer.

Maneuverability is just as important as speed, and a penguin is particularly agile underwater. In one study, a Humboldt penguin proved that it could completely reverse its direction while traveling just a quarter of its body length, a mere six inches (15 cm). The penguin could achieve this remarkable feat even when swimming at maximum speed. A penguin uses its feet, tail and laterally flattened beak as steering devices, and it's the combination of all three that gives this bird such extraordinary underwater agility.

Penguins need maneuverability not only to catch their fast-swimming prey but also to escape from predators. Under most circumstances, sharks can fin faster than penguins, and sea lions and fur seals can sprint at 14 miles per hour (22.5 km/h). Remarkably, bull killer whales can accelerate to 34 miles per hour (55 km/h). It's quite clear that without their special skills, most pursued penguins would soon be dead penguins.

Porpoising is another tactic that many penguins use to keep from becoming somebody's dinner. In porpoising, a penguin combines underwater sprints with low-level aerial leaps. This method of travel confuses underwater predators. When a penguin arcs out of the water, it is momentarily lost from view to a pursuer. Once the bird dives in again,

Many penguin species, including this gentoo, porpoise through the water whenever they leave or approach the shoreline. By diving in and out of the water, the birds become more difficult for predatory seals and killer whales to catch.

it often makes a sudden change in its direction of travel. This surprises a predator and gains the penguin a brief advantage. After this happens a few times, the predator frequently abandons the chase.

Dive, Dive, Dive

Although penguins are accomplished swimmers, diving is what they do better than any other seabird. Most penguin species can reach depths of 300 feet (90 m) and stay submerged for five to six minutes. More commonly, however, they remain underwater for just a minute or two and dive no deeper than 150 feet (45 m). The diving records are held by the largest penguins, the kings and the emperors. Kings have been recorded at depths of 1,060 feet (325 m), and big-bodied emperors can plunge to 1,755 feet (535 m) and stay submerged for up to 18 minutes.

Just for comparison, the depth record held by a human skin diver is 410 feet (125 m), and the diver held his breath for just two minutes and nine seconds. Other deep divers include the leatherback turtle—the largest living sea turtle —which hunts jellyfish to depths of 3,900 feet (1,190 m), and the bull sperm whale, which stalks bottom-dwelling sharks 10,000 feet (3,050 m) down. Remarkably, a hunting sperm whale may remain submerged for nearly two hours.

All the deep divers I have just mentioned, including penguins, breathe air. To remain submerged, deep divers must bring extra oxygen with them, stored in their lungs, blood and muscles. When scientists analyzed the extra oxygen in the lungs, air sacs, blood and muscles of king and emperor penguins, they were puzzled. There simply was not enough oxygen for the birds to stay submerged for as long as they did. Hot new research may have finally solved the mystery.

Penguins can dive deeper and remain underwater longer than any other family of birds. A typical Adélie penguin can reach depths of 300 feet (90 m) and stay under for five minutes or more.

Deep-diving penguins chill out. During a deep dive, a king penguin allows the cold water in which it is swimming to drain heat from its body so that the temperature inside its abdomen drops from a normal 102 degrees F (39°C) to an unbelievable 52 degrees F (11°C). Chilling its body core reduces the amount of oxygen the penguin burns. As a result, the extra oxygen it stores in its lungs, air sacs, blood and muscles lasts longer, and the penguin can stay underwater for a greater length of time. Exciting discoveries like these have fueled my lifelong passion for the study of animal behavior.

Not only is a penguin able to dive deeply, but it is able to do it over and over again. On a typical feeding trip, a penguin may make a remarkable number of dives. A king penguin searching for lanternfish may dive 144 times in a day, and a krill-catching macaroni may go under 244 times in only 12 hours. As far as I know, the record number of dives is held by a gentoo penguin that made 460 dives in just 15 hours. That's roughly one dive every two minutes.

Human pearl divers in the South Pacific—many of them only 12 or 13 years old—make 40 to 60 dives in a day. But sometimes the young divers become paralyzed or die from decompression sickness. When a pearl diver makes multiple dives and does not spend enough time at the surface between dives, nitrogen accumulates in the blood, and when it reaches a certain level, bubbles form in the bloodstream. These bubbles cause the greatest damage when they block tiny blood vessels inside the brain. In theory, diving penguins should also suffer from decompression sickness. How they avoid this is yet another mystery that surrounds the lives of these fascinating flightless seabirds.

Back on the Beach

In water, a penguin can change direction in a heartbeat, rocket six feet (2 m) into the air to reach the safety of an iceberg and dive to crushing depths. On land, however, the penguin turns competence into comedy, as it waddles, hops and toboggans. A penguin's legs are as far back on its body as they can be without falling off. In this position, legs are ideal as an underwater rudder, but it's a different story entirely when their owner hits the shore. On land, you might say that a penguin sways more than walks, rocking from side to side like an old sailor home from the sea. And the fatter it is, the more it sways.

I once laughed as a plumped-up king penguin came ashore. The bird could barely stand up. As soon as it took a few steps forward, it would lose its balance and fall on its belly, ramming its beak

I have watched rockhopper penguins leap off a six-foot (2 m) ledge, bounce like a spring and land safely on their bellies. This toughness enables rockhoppers to come ashore along wave-battered coastlines where other penguins would not dare to try.

into the wet sand. The tuckered-out king finally gave up and fell asleep on the beach. Perhaps a few days of dieting would make life easier?

In early spring, an Adélie penguin may have to walk 60 miles (95 km) or more over rough sea ice to reach its nesting colony on the shore. An emperor may face a trek of 120 miles (195 km) for a similar goal. For both penguins, that's a long way to waddle and sway. Emperors and Adélies have devised a way to lessen the labor of such a journey: They lie down on the job and toboggan. Flopping onto their bellies, they slide forward using their flippers for balance and the long claws on their toes for traction. Tobogganing saves the penguins considerable energy, and if several of them follow each other beak-to-tail, the bellies of those in the lead can wear a track in the snow and make the going that much easier for those in the rear.

Another way a penguin gets around on land is by hopping, and the well-named rockhopper does this better than all others. Seabird specialist Robert Cushman Murphy wrote: "Picture a penguin with a yellow pompon over each eye and a gait that caused the early visitors to the Falklands to dub it the 'Jumping Jack.' Instead of walking, it progresses in a series of bounds executed with an elasticity of motion such as is exhibited by a kangaroo." The rockhopper, the smallest of the crested penguins, may not have size, but it certainly has perseverance. Some rockhoppers may climb 500 feet (150 m) up rocky cliffs and steep slopes to reach their nesting colony, making the difficult trip one six-inch (15 cm) hop at a time. On Steeple Jason Island in the Falklands, the claws of countless climbing rockhoppers have scratched deep grooves into the rocks.

When the lead Adélie penguin in this group of tobogganers saw me, it came to a complete stop. The others were following too closely behind to apply the brakes and avoid what quickly became a four-Adélie pileup.

CHAPTER 3

WHAT'S ON THE MENU?

Penguins, like most seabirds, are strictly meat-eaters, and their diet consists of just three kinds of seafood: fish, squid and crustaceans, including krill, a shrimp look-alike. Even so, their menu is more varied than it might seem. For example, little penguins in Australia eat 28 different fish, and some African penguins dine on 18 kinds of crustaceans and 25 different fish.

In the past, there was only one way for a scientist to learn what a penguin eats—kill the bird and examine the contents of its stomach. Nowadays, a researcher simply catches the penguin, threads a hollow tube down its throat and flushes out the bird's stomach. As an emergency doctor, I did this same thing many times to patients who had taken drug overdoses. Certainly, no one ever enjoyed the procedure, but it's harmless. I expect that penguins are no different. Flushing a penguin's stomach steals a meal from the bird but causes no physical injury, although the psychological trauma of being restrained by a fuzzy-faced scientist having a bad-hair day may cause the bird to steer clear of humans forever afterward.

Once researchers flush the slimy stomach soup from a penguin, how do they sort out the goo? Luckily, the outer skeletons of most crustaceans are made of chitin, a stiff, tough material that is hard to digest. As a result, a crustacean can be identified long after it has been eaten. Identifying fish and squid is even easier. The scales of fish and the inner ear bones of squid, called otoliths, are composed of dense calcium, so they are likewise very resistant to digestion and can be used for identification many days after a meal is swallowed. Squid provide yet another clue to their identity. The sharp, horny beak that squid use to bite and kill their prey is unaffected by penguin stomach acid, and the size of the beak can be used to estimate the squid's body size. From this, scientists have determined that emperor penguins sometimes tackle two-foot-long (60 cm) squid.

I've watched thousands of penguins but have never flushed a penguin's stomach. Even so, there is another way to discover what a penguin has been eating, and that is to examine the goo *after* it leaves the penguin. The color of penguin droppings, called guano, varies as the bird's menu changes. A diet of fish pro-

As in all penguins, the gentoo's tongue and the roof of its mouth are covered with stiff spines that help it hold onto the slippery, slimy fish, krill and squid it likes to eat.

duces white or gray droppings. Krill, a shrimp-like crustacean, yields pink poop, and penguin-processed squid is yellow. A penguin that has been fasting for more than a few days has green, bile-stained guano. Streaks of colored guano radiate out from the edges of most penguin nests. You probably wouldn't think of calling a penguin an artist unless you'd seen them pucker and let the guano fly. Author Murray Levick, who may have spent a little too much time pondering penguin poop, wrote: "The excreta of Adélies…are squirted clear of the [nests] for a distance of a foot or more so that each nest has the appearance of a flower with bright green petals radiating from its center."

In the Falkland Islands, I learned that the splatter zone sometimes extends to the nest of a neighbor. Even so, the birds do not seem too disturbed when they get pasted. One rockhopper I watched was within range when its neighbor let the guano go. The rockhopper took a full shot in the face. The plastered penguin simply shook its head, snorted and let the wet goo slowly drip from its beak and golden crest.

The color of guano can signal a sudden change in a penguin's diet. On a recent trip to Antarctica, I visited a colony of chinstrap penguins that were incubating eggs on the island of South Georgia. The birds were filthy and badly soiled with dried guano of two different colors: fresh pink splattered over white. Clearly, the diet of the chinstraps had changed in a matter of weeks, from fish earlier in the season to krill.

Chasing the Chow

While it's interesting to know what penguins eat, it is even more interesting to learn how they catch their food. When penguins leave a colony on a feeding trip, they commonly travel in groups of 10 to 30 birds. However, once they reach the area they want to search, they usually split into singles, pairs and trios. But even when three or four penguins remain together, they hunt as individuals and do not cooperate in locating or catching prey, as do killer whales and some birds of prey, among others.

Penguins are visual hunters and rely primarily on their eyesight to find food. Their eyes are not particularly large, nor do they have any special reflective layers behind the retinas to amplify the light, as do owls and other nocturnal animals. As a result, penguins are mainly daytime hunters, feeding during the middle hours of the day when the sun is highest in the

A good penguin watcher can tell what a bird has been eating by the color of its guano. The chinstrap, **top**, is splattered with pink poop sprayed from neighbors eating krill, whereas the whitewashed gentoo, **bottom**, has fish-eating neighbors.

sky. At this time, the light penetrates deepest into the water.

In the ocean, sunlight usually never reaches deeper than 650 feet (200 m), yet as we have seen, king and emperor penguins dive well beyond these depths. How do the deep divers find their prey in the total darkness? The answer is bioluminescence. Many squid and crustaceans and some of the fish that penguins hunt have luminous spots scattered over their bodies. These spots flash and glow in the dark, and penguins probably use them to locate their prey.

Most of the prey that penguins hunt occur in clumps made up of many individuals. Schools of anchovies, for example, may contain thousands of these small fish, and swarms of krill sometimes number in the millions. Immense "super-swarms" of krill may redden the surface of the ocean for 50 square miles (130 km^2) and extend 325 feet (100 m) down. If you were to dip a water pitcher into such a dense swarm, you would catch hundreds of krill. Multiply that by tens of millions, and you have some idea of how many krill there are in such a swarm.

The challenge for a penguin is to locate the swarms and schools scattered over the vastness of the ocean. As a result, a hunting penguin may search a long time before it finally finds food, but by then, it is a skilled predator. Banded penguins that prey mainly on schools

Once a banded penguin, such as this magellanic, finds a school of fish, it circles them repeatedly, packing them into a dense group. The crafty penguin then rockets through the school from below, snatching up one fish after another.

of fish have a special technique for catching their quarry. All four species of banded penguins have black-and-white stripes on their flanks, and this bold pattern may startle the fish when the bird circles them. A penguin's tactic is to circle a school repeatedly, bunching the fish tighter and tighter together. Eventually, the fish are packed so tightly that the coordination of the school breaks down. When this happens, the fish get confused and flee in all directions. And that's when the penguin strikes. Diving beneath the school, it swims through it from below, grabbing the frightened fish, one after another. The dark plumage of a penguin's back seen from above against the depths of the ocean hides the bird's approach until it is too late for the prey to react.

Penguins catch their prey one at a time. When the prey is small, they swallow it underwater and continue fishing. In this way, a gentoo may capture 100 krill in a single dive, and a king penguin may nab more than 25 lanternfish before it returns to the surface to breathe. To help the penguin swallow slippery, wiggly prey, the upper surface of its tongue and the roof of its mouth are covered with stiff spines that face inward. There is only one direction for the food to go—inside the guano machine.

Not everything a penguin swallows wiggles and squirms. Sometimes, penguins eat rocks. I once followed a parade of chinstraps as they waddled from their nesting colony back to the ocean. Along the way, two of the birds each picked up a small pebble from the path and carried it in its beak. When they finally disappeared into the surf, each penguin still had the pebble clamped in its mouth. Many species of penguins have stones in their stomachs; a large emperor may carry a pound (450 g) of them.

The whalers and sealers of the 1800s were convinced that penguins swallowed stones to help them control their buoyancy, but modern scientists still have no satisfactory explanation for this behavior. Nonetheless, it was a penguin's appetite for pebbles that suggested the existence of Antarctica before the continent was discovered. In 1840, an American expedition captured an emperor penguin at 66 degrees 52 minutes south latitude, just inside the Antarctic Circle. When the penguin's stomach was dissected, the sailors were surprised to find pebbles of basalt, a volcanic rock. They reasoned that the bird must have traveled from some unknown land. They were right.

Feeding the Kids

Scientists estimate that on an average day, a penguin will stuff itself with seafood amounting to about 20 percent of its own body weight. I weigh 190 pounds (85 kg), and if I did the same, I would need to gobble and gulp my way through 38 pounds (15 kg) of food. A penguin may eat even more when it has a chick to feed. In such cases, some Adélies may load up with 40,000 krill. A magellanic penguin in Argentina

A newly hatched Adélie chick plunges its head completely inside its parent's throat for dinner. In this way, no food is spilled and wasted. This method also prevents gulls and other birds from stealing the chick's food.

was caught with 22 squid in its gut. The squid weighed a belly-bursting nine pounds (4 kg), nearly the same weight as the bird itself.

A penguin chick rarely needs urging to eat. As soon as a parent returns to the nest, a chick starts to chirp. The young bird stimulates the adult to feed it by rapidly vibrating its beak against that of its parent. When the adult bird opens its mouth, the chick wedges its bill inside and gobbles up the slimy goo. The head of a small chick may disappear completely inside a parent's throat. Typically, a chick receives 8 to 12 servings like this, feeding until the parent bird has nothing left to regurgitate. A large,

After swallowing as many fish as it can hold, the gentoo chick in front is now stuffed. Unable to manage another bite, it wanders away from the nest, allowing its sibling to finish the remainder of the meal in peace.

well-fed chinstrap chick may receive 1½ pounds (680 g) in a single meal, and a king penguin chick may gobble down 6½ pounds (3 kg), so much food that the chick looks like an over-stuffed laundry bag.

Mealtime for chicks is not always quite so orderly. The brush-tailed penguins, for example, commonly have two chicks in a family, and in these species, mealtime is just another word for food fight. When the chicks are small, the bigger of the two simply bullies its sibling and steals most of the chow. After a month or so, the hungry chicks must run for their dinner. I've watched these so-called feeding chases in gentoo penguins many times in the Falkland Islands, and this is how I described the action in my journal:

"Suddenly, the chase is on, and the adult bird appears to be running for its life, closely followed by two imploring chicks. The eagerness of the chicks can be so great that they run into the rear of the adult, stepping on its tail. I sometimes wonder whether the chicks might not keep on running right up their parent's back if the adult stopped without warning.

"The dogged chicks shadow the parent's every dodge and turn and are remarkably fast, despite their potbellied profiles. As they run along, they chirp loudly and flap their flippers limply. A chase often lasts a minute or two, with the penguins cutting through the colony in a zigzag course, along one edge and then back through the crowd again. Invariably, one of the chicks tires and drops out of the race. Shortly after that, the adult stops and allows the remaining runner to catch up if it has lagged behind.... Soon, a slimy wad of regurgitated fish slides down the parent's beak into the gape of the chick—the reward for perseverance."

CHAPTER 4

THE MATING GAME

The mating season is one of the most important yearly events in a penguin's life. For most species, the season starts in September and October, the spring months in the southern hemisphere. The activity begins when the birds, fat and full of fight, gather in crowded colonies to strut their stuff.

Penguin colonies come in three sizes: small, large and beyond belief. Almost every species has its share of small colonies, where one or two dozen pairs cluster together. In some cases, these are satellite colonies that were established when larger colonies became overpopulated. Large colonies are common among penguins. Consider the 25,000 pairs of rockhoppers in a single colony on the island of Tristan da Cunha or the 50,000 pairs of kings at Lusitania Bay on Macquarie Island. Such a concentration of bird life is truly breathtaking to witness.

Unbelievably, some penguins live life on an even larger scale: 270,000 pairs of Adélies crowd the slopes of Cape Adare on the ice-choked coast of Antarctica; 400,000 pairs of macaroni penguins cluster on Possession Island; and an astounding five million pairs of chinstraps crowd and compete on the cinder and ash of the volcanic South Sandwich Islands. In colonies of this size, the air pulsates with life.

So many beating flippers and hearts, so much noise and odor, so much sex and energy—nothing else on Earth compares with it.

Although penguin colonies differ greatly in size, the spacing between the birds is usually fairly constant for each species, even when there is room to spread out. For example, magellanic penguins typically nest in burrows three to four feet (1 m) apart, whether there are a few hundred birds or a few thousand. The large crested penguins (macaroni, royal and erect-crested species) pack themselves together with two or three pairs sharing only a square yard. Sharing is probably the wrong word, since the bad-tempered birds squabble and fight continually. They actually space themselves just beyond pecking distance of each other. The tightest squeeze occurs with emperor penguins. In a single square yard of colony, 8 to 10 big, bulky birds stand shoulder to shoulder. As I discussed earlier, these penguins need to share body heat with each other, so they cannot

Looking like a Coney Island beach in midsummer, the king penguin colony at Salisbury Plain on South Georgia is one of the great wildlife spectacles of the world. At peak numbers, there may be over 40,000 resident penguins.

afford to spread out. Instead, emperors are forced to be sociable. At the other end of the scale are the yellow-eyed penguins, the least sociable of the 17 species. Penguins in yellow-eyed colonies, if you could call them colonies at all, nest 50 to 150 yards (45-135 m) apart. Yellow-eyes don't seem to mind *listening* to the neighbors; they just don't want to *see* them. In fact, if two nesting pairs can see each other, one or both of the pairs will abandon the nest.

Penguin colonies can be very old. Renowned bird artist Roger Tory Peterson called penguin colonies "ancient graveyards," built on the bones and guano of countless generations of breeding birds. Some Adélie colonies in Antarctica

may be several thousand years old, and one macaroni colony on Marion Island has been in use for at least 7,000 years.

The obvious question is, Why are penguins so colony-crazy? To begin with, penguins may crowd together simply because there is a shortage of suitable nesting locations. In Antarctica, for example, less than 3 percent of the continent is free of ice and snow during the summer months, so the chinstraps, gentoos and Adélies that nest there have little choice but to cram together. A shortage of space, however, does not explain why most penguins cluster in colonies.

Many seabird biologists think that there are at least four other reasons colonies are so

Competition for real estate is fierce in Antarctica, where very little land is free of ice and snow during the summer. Nevertheless, 99 percent of Adélie penguins return each year to breed in the same colony where they hatched.

attractive to nesting penguins. First, when penguins nest close together, predators such as gulls and skuas find it harder to land and walk between the nests and to stay outside the pecking range of neighboring penguins.

Another reason to court and breed in colonies is to share information, particularly about the location of food. Swarms of squid, krill and fish are often scattered over the ocean and are therefore difficult to locate. A few penguins searching separately may easily miss such prey. When an entire colony of penguins is hunting over the same area, however, there is a much better chance that at least some of the birds will discover where the food is concentrated. Once they have done so, other members of the colony can follow these birds to the food source.

A third benefit of living in a colony is that it encourages the mating mood. Penguins calling and courting together seem to stimulate one another with their behavior. For example, it is well known that colonial seabirds court and mate more frequently when they are surrounded by neighbors who are also courting. In addition, seabirds in large groups lay their eggs sooner than those in small groups. In short, noisy crowds stimulate hormone levels in these birds and modify their behavior in a beneficial way.

Finally, in most penguin colonies, the majority of chicks hatch at roughly the same time. The sudden arrival of large numbers of young, vulnerable birds saturates the environment of the local predators with potential prey. The larger the number of chicks, the less damage predators can do to the colony's total population.

Property Problems

A penguin can live for 20 years or more. With such long lives, most penguins do not begin to breed until they are 3 or 4 years old, and some of the large crested species may not breed until they are 8 or 9. No matter how old they are, though, penguins typically start their love lives in their home colony. Young Adélies probably stray the least of any species. Ninety-nine percent nest in the same colony where they started life inside an egg, and three-quarters of them do so within 200 yards (185 m) of where they hatched.

At the beginning of the breeding season, male penguins usually arrive at the nesting site a week or so before the females. Returning to a colony is no guarantee that a penguin will automatically inherit a piece of prime property. The best sites are quickly taken, although often

Young adult rockhoppers will return to a colony for several years in a row before they eventually begin to nest. In that time, the birds mature and gain valuable life skills in courtship, defending a territory and nest building.

33

not without a struggle. When the success or failure of breeding is at stake, male penguins are ready to fight.

Penguins are tough birds with thick skin, strong beaks and stiff, bony flippers, and the battles they wage can be surprisingly violent. Many fights are bill-wrestling, chest-bumping, flipper-bashing brawls that end only when both contestants are completely exhausted. The fighters tear at each other with their sharp beaks, and the birds can be left covered with blood. Worse than that, some may be blinded.

I watched a pair of chinstraps battle over the ownership of a prime nest located in the center of a small colony. The warriors beat each other repeatedly with their sturdy flippers as they fought their way through four or five other nesting territories. Having reached the edge of the colony, the penguins continued to thrash and tear at each other across 30 yards (25 m) of gravel beach. The war ended at the water's edge when one of the birds escaped into the surf. The males had battled for nearly five minutes, and the winner's left flipper was dripping with blood. As he waddled back to the colony to claim his prize nest, however, he seemed barely affected by the fight. He had victory to give him strength, and now he was a landowner.

Once a male has won a nest site, the first thing he does is scream about it to the neighbors. The triumphant calls of male penguins have been described as trumpeting, braying and hoarse wheezing. But by any name, all are loud and harsh. Often, as soon as one male begins to scream, all the penguins around him also scream—a kind of penguin shouting match that may gradually spread throughout the entire colony. Biologists have named these male bragging bouts "ecstatic calls," a way for a penguin

As in most penguin colonies, the spacing between neighbors in a gentoo colony is nearly always the same. The birds like to be just far enough apart to be out of pecking and slapping range of each other.

to advertise not only his ownership of a nesting site but his interest in meeting any female looking for a mate.

Male penguins are not choosy; they will court any female penguin with flippers. Even so, 60 to 90 percent of penguins end up with the same mate they had the previous season. Although penguins rarely mate for life, most macaroni penguins reunite for at least four breeding seasons, and some pairs of yellow-eyes stay with the same mate for up to 13 years.

In the past, biologists, most of whom were men, thought that the male penguins did all the choosing and the female simply accepted whichever male showed an interest in her. Today, researchers believe that female penguins make the final choice of mate, and they can be very picky. Even when a female joins the same partner she had the previous year, she may still assess his qualities to make sure he is a suitable mate.

A female can measure the worth of a male partner in at least two ways—by his color and by his voice. The bright colors on the head, neck and beak of a penguin can be an indication of the bird's health. A bird infected with internal parasites, for example, may be weak and the colors on its body dull and washed out. A female penguin with a sharp eye can use the appearance of the feathers to measure the vitality of a potential mate. When inquisitive scientists used shoe polish to blacken the bright orange ear patches on adult male king penguins, the males were unable to attract a mate. Even the other males in the colony ignored these males and never treated them as rivals.

The female also listens to a potential partner's voice; if it sounds too high, she may look elsewhere for a mate. The tone of a male's ecstatic call is influenced by the size of his body and by how fat he is. The call of a fat male with a big body is lower in tone than the call of a slimmer bird. A human cannot hear the difference, but a female penguin certainly can. Big, fat males are attractive because their robust condition indicates that they can forage well and can fast for a long period and incubate the eggs while the female hunts at sea. In the end, female penguins not only look their mates over but listen closely to their love songs as well.

Burrows, Nests & Bare Feet

Once a female penguin settles down with a partner, the pair begins to build a nest. Penguins live in such a wide range of habitats, from the equator to Antarctica, it is not surprising that the various species build different kinds of nests. The little penguin and the four banded penguins live in the warmest climates. All these species nest in rock crevices, under bushes or in burrows, where their eggs and young are shielded from the worst heat of the sun.

Some burrows may be more than three feet (90 cm) deep. In the past, many banded pen-

Most of the crested penguins, including this macaroni, build simple nests of dried grasses, which quickly become trampled by the parents as they incubate their eggs.

guins dug their burrows into the thick layers of guano that had accumulated in the colonies. On the Chincha Islands, off the coast of Peru, for example, the guano was 180 feet (55 m) deep. Guano is a rich fertilizer, and humans have collected it for centuries, sometimes by the shipload. In the late 1800s, many of the Humboldt and African penguins had their nesting sites dug up and removed. Today, dried guano is still collected, but in most places, enough is left behind for the penguins to dig their burrows.

Penguins that nest in burrows often haul in dried grass, twigs and molted feathers to line the nesting chamber. Cherry Kearton describes how African penguins pad their burrows: "I have seen penguins with long, trailing bits of seaweed struggling up the slope from the sea— a matter, as often as not, of half a mile or more —the seaweed becoming entangled in their legs and nearly tripping them up."

Some penguins are not as fussy, and when seaweed and grass are not available, they use whatever trash they can find. In the burrows of magellanic penguins, researchers have uncovered small mammal bones, paper litter, the skulls of songbirds, chips of dried cattle manure and the dried pelts of dead penguins. Hoping to find something equally interesting, I once crawled down the burrow of a magellanic penguin in the Falkland Islands and found nothing

The Adélie penguin on the right has just been relieved of its egg-sitting duties by its well-fed mate. As a final gesture before leaving to feed at sea, the liberated parent adds a pebble to the nest.

but grass and biting fleas. My interest in penguin burrows ended very quickly.

In the colder climates, most penguins build their nests on top of the ground, because a cool burrow is not necessary to protect young chicks from the heat of the sun. Gentoos in the Falklands gather clumps of earth and build six-inch-high (15 cm) mounds. On Macquarie Island, one royal penguin made a nest pile entirely of old bleached penguin bones. Adélies and chinstraps are the rock masons of the penguin world, building piles of pebbles for their nests.

There are definite benefits to building a nest, even when it is only an inch or two high. A nest raises the eggs off the cold, sometimes frozen ground, and as a result, the eggs stay warmer. An elevated nest can also protect eggs and young chicks from flooding. If the nest is not big enough, however, the meltwater from a late-spring snowstorm can drown chicks and flush eggs right out of the nest. In the life of a penguin, nest material is valuable, and anything that is valuable is worth stealing.

Penguins are incurable thieves, and a nest owner may be a victim one moment and a robber the next. I have watched penguins steal from each other many times, and it's always entertaining. As soon as a nesting bird nods off for a nap, the neighbors may come calling. A penguin with theft on its mind quietly waddles up to a likely

Racing through the colony like an urban purse snatcher outrunning the police, this gentoo penguin carries a stolen wad of nesting material back to its own nest, which its partner is guarding.

nest. If the nest owner is sleeping or looking the other way, the pebble pirate slowly leans forward, quickly grabs a stone and then runs off as if its tail were on fire. If the thief is caught in the act, it may be punished with a hard peck or a whack with a flipper, but that doesn't seem to discourage the culprit. A penguin often tries time and time again until it eventually succeeds. One early penguin researcher painted pebbles bright red and left a pile of them near a colony of Adélies. Within hours, the stone stealing started. After three days, the red pebbles had been looted from one nest to the next and carried throughout the colony.

In 1995, a trio of Spanish researchers watched stone stealing in a colony of chinstraps and made some interesting discoveries. Although both males and females made off with stones from neighboring nests, the male collected larger stones, wandered farther afield to do it and stole more stones than did its female partner. The nests of some pairs tripled in weight during the nesting season, sometimes weighing in at up to 23 pounds (10 kg) and containing over 600 pebbles. Other nests shrank by as much as 70 percent and contained as few as 36 pebbles. The researchers concluded that experienced high-ranking males build the largest nests and defend them best. Low-ranking males, on the other hand, are neither able to defend their nests nor able to collect enough stones to offset theft by their neighbors.

Two penguins, the king and the emperor, never have to worry about having their nests stolen from under them—they simply carry their eggs with them. Both kings and emperors lay a single egg. Within moments of the egg's being laid, one of the parents rolls it onto the top of its feet and covers it with a fold of its feathered belly skin. After that, no matter where the parent moves, the egg is always with it. In king penguins, the male and female partners take turns holding and warming the egg. In emperor penguins, the male cradles the egg on its feet for the entire incubation period, which lasts 64 days. The devoted father never lets the egg leave the top of its feet. If ever a penguin deserved the title "Mr. Mom," it's the male emperor.

The Egg Beat

After the penguins pair up, they settle down at a nest, steal a few pebbles for each other, then start to get serious, and the mating begins. When you are shaped like a football, that's harder to do than it sounds. While watching

This magellanic penguin, **top**, constructed its nest at the end of a three-foot-long (90 cm) tunnel, where its eggs and young will be protected from harsh temperatures as well as predators. The benefits of the large nest built by this experienced dominant chinstrap penguin, **bottom**, are evident: Eggs and chicks are elevated off the frozen ground, and the nest is much less likely to flood.

several pairs of rockhoppers mate, I recorded these observations in my journal:

"Once the female is sprawled invitingly on her belly, the male hops up onto her back and slowly treads backwards. A mounted male reminds me of an excited youngster trying to balance on a skateboard. He nibbles the feathers on his partner's crown and neck, wags his tail from side to side and slaps her flanks with his flippers, like a cowboy urging his horse on.... It has been raining for the last couple of days, and all the females have muddy tread marks on their backs."

A penguin pair may start to mate several weeks before the first egg is laid, and as the time of laying draws closer, the birds mate as often as 12 to 14 times a day. Typically, all penguins (except kings and emperors) lay two white eggs that quickly become stained with mud and guano. Penguin eggs have thicker shells than the eggs of most seabirds, which protects them from their clumsy waddling parents, the beaks of grumpy neighbors and the sharp stones that line many nests.

In all species but emperors, both parents share in incubating the eggs, although the shift schedule differs among the species. In gentoos and the banded species, for example, the mates alternate frequently, usually relieving each other every few days. In Adélies, chinstraps and the crested penguins, each sex starts with a long incubation shift lasting between 7 and 14 days, after which the partners change over more frequently as the time of hatching draws closer. In all cases, while one parent incubates, the other heads out to sea to feed and build up its fat reserves again.

One amusing penguin behavior is the "slender walk" of an adult returning to relieve its mate. In large colonies containing several thousand birds, a returning penguin may have to cross the territories of over a hundred bad-tempered neighbors with sharp beaks. All penguin species that nest together in such numbers use this special walk to pass through the crowd with as few pecks and flipper whacks as possible. In Adélies, for example, the bird flattens its feathers to make itself as slim as possible, stretches its flippers behind its back, raises its beak skyward, then runs a zigzag course for home. Returning penguins are usually silent, but their body language sends a clear message: Just passing through... sorry to disturb you... no fights, please.

When you are shaped like a football, as these king penguins are, **top**, mating can be a real balancing act. The eggs of all penguins, including this gentoo, **bottom**, have very thick shells. This prevents accidental breakage as clumsy adults shuffle around the nest.

The urge to incubate must be strong in penguins, because they often nest in very difficult conditions. During a storm in the Falklands, I hiked to a gentoo colony to see what the birds have to put up with. It was raining hard, and the wind was gusting to 45 miles per hour (70 km/h). The birds were huddled over their nests with their eyes closed, facing into the wind. What impressed me most was that every bird was completely caked in mud except for its beak.

Snowstorms can be another hardship for penguin parents. On the Antarctic Peninsula, late-spring storms can completely bury an incubating bird, leaving only its head visible above the snow. If an Adélie is buried like this for more than three days, the stress is too much for the bird, and it will desert the nest.

The biggest stress for many incubating penguins is the fasting. Some incubating shifts may last for two weeks or more. Add to that weeks of fasting during courtship and nest building, and some parent penguins may not eat for a period of six weeks. Remarkably, male emperor penguins may not eat for three months. Incubating birds rely on their fat reserves to provide energy while they are fasting, and they may lose up to half of their body weight. These fat reserves can run out, however, and if a mate stays at sea too long and is late relieving its partner, the incubating bird has no choice but to abandon the eggs and flee to the sea to feed.

Flipper-Flapping Fluffies

The eggs of most penguin species hatch after 35 to 40 days. Naturally, it is longer in the two largest species: king penguins incubate for 54 days, emperors for 64 days. Shortly before an egg begins to crack, the tiny chick can be heard chirping inside the shell. Because the eggshell is so thick, it may take as long as three days for a chick to struggle free. The incubating parents never interfere, although they often look down at the egg and seem very interested in what is happening. Sometimes, a parent even regurgitates gobs of food onto the egg.

Newly hatched penguin chicks are covered with fine down, ranging in color from silver-gray to dark brown or black, depending on the species. At this age, the chicks' eyelids are sealed shut, and like so many young nestlings, they are puny wobbly-necked bags of fluff that peep constantly to be fed.

The bare area on the belly of this Adélie penguin is known as the brood patch. At the start of the breeding season, the feathers are lost from this spot, allowing the parent to transfer body heat more directly to the egg. Once the egg is hatched, the feathers grow back.

During the first weeks of a penguin chick's life, it is continually guarded by one of its parents. Depending on the size of the penguin, the guarding phase lasts anywhere from two to eight weeks. While one parent stands guard, the other hunts for food to feed the cheeping chick. The helpless chick needs to be guarded against three main dangers: the weather, the neighbors and predators.

The temperature on a summer day in Antarctica may be just 40 degrees F (4.5°C), which is cold enough to kill chicks. The down-feather coat on young chinstraps and Adélies is too thin for them to maintain their own body temperatures. Until they are several weeks

old, they huddle under the warmth of a parent's belly fold, stare out and watch the world go by. Penguin chicks grow rapidly, and within a few weeks, they have ballooned into potbellied little tubbies that no longer fit under a parent, so they simply squat beside the adult bird like miniature Buddhas waiting to be fed—and fed again.

The weather can kill young penguins even at this stage of their growth. Cold and blowing snow can freeze the chicks in their tracks. One Christmas in the Falkland Islands, an icy rain battered a rockhopper colony for more than 24 hours. Nearly half of the chicks in the colony died during the storm. The young penguins, soaked by the rain, were too big for their parents to cover and warm, and when the cold winds slowly drained away all their body heat, they froze to death.

Neighbors can sometimes be just as dangerous as the weather. In most colonies, there is usually much less squabbling among the adults by the time the chicks begin to hatch. Even so, occasional fights still break out, and young nestlings can be injured during the ruckus. A tiny bird can be trampled, punctured with a toenail, kicked and blinded or knocked from a nest into a neighbor's territory. I watched the fate of one defenseless rockhopper chick that was kicked from its nest while its parent was fighting. I recorded the incident in my field notes:

"The neighbor adults stretched over and screamed a loud threat at the tiny chick, and then the big-beaked male attacked. He shook the chick vigorously and gave it six or seven hard pecks on the body and head, killing it very quickly. The aggressive male continued to peck at the chick periodically for 10 minutes after it was dead."

Every penguin colony attracts a squad of predators looking for an easy meal. In the Galá-

A bevy of chicks: A king penguin chick, **facing page**, looks like a plush overstuffed toy; the beaks on this pair of Adélie chicks, **top**, each sport the white egg tooth the chicks used to break out of their shells; the rockhopper chick, **bottom**, gets the full-time attention of both parents for its first month.

pagos Islands, crimson-shelled Sally lightfoot crabs will drag off a tiny struggling chick and eat it alive. In Australia, there are venomous tiger snakes; in Argentina and Chile, gray foxes and Geoffroy's cats; and in Africa, needle-toothed mongooses. The greatest threat to young penguin chicks, however, is other birds—gulls, skuas and giant petrels—all of which are bold and clever predators. The killing tactics they use will be described in the next chapter.

About a month after hatching, most penguin chicks have grown large enough to be left temporarily on their own. Both parents can now go out to sea and thereby deliver twice as many meals. The behavior of unguarded chicks differs among the various species. In the burrow- and crevice-nesting banded penguins and the little penguin, the chicks tend to be homebodies, hanging out by themselves or with their nest-mates at the mouth of their burrows. The chicks of most of the other species herd together in sizable groups called crèches—gangs of pot-bellied, flat-footed, flipper-flapping fluffies.

Penguin crèches vary in size. Many of the crested species clump together in groups of 20 to 30 chicks. Downy Adélies can form clusters of 100 or more, and big, brown, fuzzy king penguin chicks may gather in immense crèches of 1,000 birds. Initially, a crèche may contain just two or three chicks, but it can grow larger very quickly. In one Adélie colony containing several thousand nesting pairs, the first chicks were left unguarded on December 30. Eleven days later, all but 1 percent of the chicks had joined crèches.

When the first chicks in a colony begin to form crèches, there are still many adults guarding smaller chicks. The adults are aggressive around their nests and may peck any careless chick that wanders too near. Because of this,

the clusters of chicks usually form on the edge of a colony or, better yet, in an unoccupied area in the center of a colony, where they are surrounded by adult birds that can shield them from predators. Unguarded chicks gather in crèches for two reasons: There is safety in numbers, and a cluster of hot-blooded chicks is a good place to snuggle into when cold winds blow.

In many species, when a parent returns to the colony to feed its chicks, it may be mobbed by half a dozen hungry beaks. In the past, biologists thought that an adult penguin would feed whichever chick happened to reach it first and beg for food. But now we know that penguins, like just about every other animal on Earth, feed only their own offspring. How does an adult penguin

Whenever a young gentoo chick is frightened, whether by a low-flying gull or an aggressive neighbor, it flattens itself on the ground and hides its head under the closest parent.

44

identify its chicks? It listens to the chirps.

Penguin chicks begin to chirp even before they hatch, and once they are out of the shell, they call all the time. In fact, a parent can quiet a chick in only one of two ways: feed it until it bulges, or sit on top of it. At first, a chick's voice sounds much like that of the chicks in the other nests around it. Slowly, however, it develops a distinctive call different from that of any other chick. For young Adélies, this happens by the time the chick is about 3 weeks old. By then, the parents have memorized its call, and they remember it for as long as they care for the chick.

Chicks also memorize the hoarse shrieks of their parents. When a parent penguin returns from the ocean to feed its chicks, it usually goes back to its nest. As it gets close to home, it trumpets and screams that it is coming. As soon as a chick hears its parent, it leaves the crèche and hurries back to its old nest to be fed. Curious researchers used tape recordings of adult calls to lure Adélie chicks out of the crèche. In almost every case, the correct Adélie chick—and only that chick—left the security of the crèche and waddled over to the nest.

Chick rearing is the longest part of the nesting cycle and is the time when young penguins as well as their parents are exposed to the greatest danger from predators. In the next chapter, we'll talk about the enemies of penguins —the ones with feathers, the ones with fur and the ones with tentacles, flukes and fins.

If a young king penguin is foolhardy enough to beg for food from an adult that is not its parent, it may get pecked, slapped with a flipper or sometimes even chased.

CHAPTER 5

PENGUIN KILLERS

Gulls are one of the most successful groups of seabirds. There are gulls on every continent, and they range from the High Arctic, just 400 miles (645 km) from the North Pole, to the shores of Antarctica. There is usually at least one species of gull wherever penguins live. One reason gulls are so successful is that they will eat almost anything, and when they are around penguins, this includes penguin poop, gobs of spilled food, fresh or rotten eggs, dead chicks and defenseless live ones.

The handsome dolphin gull is not big enough to attack a chick, but everything else is fair game. I watched a pair of dolphin gulls work a gentoo colony in the Falkland Islands. Again and again, the gulls flew low over the colony, just above the stabbing beaks of the adults, searching for discarded eggs or food that had spilled onto the ground. Another tactic was to walk around the edges of the colony and watch for parents feeding chicks. The crafty gulls sometimes worked together and rushed at the chick just as it was about to receive a gooey gob of food. This frightened the chick, and it often turned away from its parent just as the hot meal was on its way. The bold gulls then grabbed the food right out of the parent's beak or scooped it up as it hit the ground.

The kelp gull is twice as heavy as the dolphin gull and is large enough to attack penguin chicks. A strong flyer, the kelp gull can land in the middle of a penguin colony, pick up a small dead chick and fly away before the adults can catch it. The beak and feet of a gull are not designed to kill, so these birds are best at scavenging. Even so, the adaptable gulls will attack small penguin chicks and any larger chicks that are sick or dying.

Another penguin predator is the giant petrel, a 10-pound (4.5 kg) seabird with a five-inch (13 cm) butcher beak. The old-time whalers called this big seabird "stinker," partly because of its taste for rotting carcasses but more because of its habit of vomiting up foul-smelling stomach oil and spraying it on intruders up to six feet (2 m) away. In the subantarctic islands of New Zealand, I once got too close to a giant petrel chick with my camera, and the chick sprayed my jeans with a jet of oily goo that smelled so bad, I had to throw the pants away.

A giant petrel is big enough to tackle even a

The vultures of the southern oceans, giant petrels scavenge any dead animal they find. This bloodied bird was feeding on the carcass of an elephant seal. Giant petrels also readily attack and kill weak or injured penguins.

full-grown penguin. In Argentina, a researcher watched the struggle between a giant petrel and an adult magellanic penguin. The battle lasted for nearly 15 minutes, until finally, the exhausted petrel drowned the penguin. A magellanic penguin weighs as much as a petrel and is armed with an equally dangerous beak. As a result, such daring attacks on healthy adult penguins are probably quite rare.

It is a different story if the penguin is sick or injured. Many times, I have seen one or more giant petrels lying quietly on the beach near a bloodied penguin, waiting for the bird to weaken enough to be attacked. Such was the case in South Georgia when I spent an hour watching as five giant petrels surrounded an injured macaroni penguin. The penguin was soaked in blood from a severe laceration on its neck and did not look as if it would survive. Even though the penguin was very weak, the petrels did not attack it. When some tourists landed and accidentally frightened the macaroni into the water, the stinkers swarmed over the dying bird and tore it apart. Minutes later, nothing was left but the penguin's feathered skin and a pair of pink feet floating on the swell.

Skuas: Seabirds of Prey

Skuas look like gulls and are closely related to them, but they behave more like birds of prey. Their beaks are sharp-edged and hooked, they

The gentoo parents had been incubating this infertile egg for several weeks. When it was accidentally kicked out of the nest, the skua grabbed it for dinner.

have curved claws on their webbed feet, and their legs are covered with tough protective scales. Seabird expert Robert Cushman Murphy admired the skuas he saw on South Georgia, writing that "the skuas look and act like miniature eagles. They fear nothing [and] never seek to avoid being conspicuous, and by every token of their behavior, they are Lords of the Far South."

Skuas pester penguins more than any other bird does, stealing their eggs and preying on their chicks. For five years, researcher Dr. Euan Young studied the hunting tactics of a group of skuas in a colony of nesting Adélie penguins. The stealthy skua uses three main methods to outwit the penguins. In a "jump attack," the skua, with wings raised, rushes and leaps at a standing penguin, striking it high on the body with its outstretched feet and knocking the bird off balance. In the excitement, an egg or small chick may be uncovered, and the fast-acting skua nabs it before the penguin can react.

A bolder maneuver is the "crash flight," in which the skua glides into a penguin. The force of the collision may push the startled penguin into its irritable neighbors, adding to the commotion. Although both the jump attack and the crash flight are successful roughly one-third of the time, they expose the skua to the high risk of injury, so neither method is used very often.

If a couple of penguins manage to grab a skua, they can do some serious damage. The penguin's stiff flippers are strong enough to break bones, and its beak is a dangerous weapon. I once watched an unfortunate skua drop into the middle of a rockhopper colony and try to snatch a small chick. It caught the chick, but then the penguins caught the skua. Half a dozen rockhoppers attacked, viciously beating it with their bony flippers and tearing at its head and body with their powerful beaks. The skua dropped the chick almost immediately but was unable to get away, because there were too many penguins pulling at its body for it to get airborne. The bird's only choice was to struggle on foot to the edge of the colony, fighting off new attackers every few feet. When the battered skua finally escaped, its left wing was drooping and it had blood on the feathers of its face. The final score for the day: penguins one, skua zero.

The more common, and safer, skua hunting tactic is to tug on a nesting penguin's tail feathers. When the bird swivels to respond, its chicks or eggs are exposed to attack. This method works even better when two skuas team up. While one bird pesters the penguin, the other grabs lunch. If a skua catches a penguin snoozing, it can sometimes jerk its tail feathers so strongly that the sleeping bird is pulled off the nest. Before the surprised penguin can react, the skua leaps over and grabs an egg or a chick.

Fin-Footed Hunters

Seals, sea lions and fur seals—the fin-footed mammals—inhabit every ocean on Earth. All are carnivores and hunt for a living, and for

A week earlier, a hailstorm pummeled this rockhopper colony, killing nearly half of the chicks. The skua, always on the lookout for a feeding opportunity, dines on one of the dead chicks.

some of them, penguins are on the menu. No sea lion or fur seal is a full-time penguin killer, but in many areas, they may hunt penguins when an opportunity arises. During the nesting season, adult penguins are moving back and forth from their colonies to the ocean every few days, if not more often. When they return from long feeding trips, the birds are tired, weighted down with food and easier to catch. Sea lions and fur seals, especially juvenile males, often station themselves offshore from large penguin colonies and hunt the birds, not only for food but sometimes for sport.

I watched a young male South American sea lion catch and kill two king penguins on a beach in the Falkland Islands. Although the sea lion ate part of the first penguin, it ate none of the second. The animal played in the surf with the second king for several minutes, even tossing the flapping bird into the air. Once the penguin was dead, the sea lion submerged with the bird's body in its mouth a couple of times and then abandoned the carcass. A dozen giant petrels, attracted by the commotion in the water, made certain that no scrap was wasted.

The fin-footed penguin killer that ranks above all others is the 900-pound (400 kg) leopard seal of the Antarctic. In one year, a dozen leopard seals hunting at the large Adélie colony at Cape Crozier killed 4,800 adults and 1,200 chicks. Young penguins moving into the water on their first trip to sea are easy prey; they are literally sitting penguins. The inexperienced Adélies are completely unaware of the danger from a leopard seal. A curious youngster may even swim over to a seal that is floating quietly on the surface. Snap. Another lesson learned.

Adult Adélies are much warier and harder to catch. Even so, leopard seals in some areas manage to kill 5 percent of the adult penguins in a colony. That doesn't sound like very many penguins until you remember that some colonies have 200,000 breeding birds. The leopard seal toll at one of those colonies would be 10,000 penguins.

Leopard seals use a number of strategies to hunt penguins. One is to stalk the birds from under thin ice. With this method, an underwater seal follows a penguin walking across newly formed ice, breaks through the ice (which can be up to three inches/7.5 cm thick) and grabs the unsuspecting bird. If a penguin spots a seal before it attacks, the bird may freeze with fear, remaining motionless for over an hour until it feels safe enough to continue.

Leopard seals also leap onto ice floes and try to snatch any careless penguin that is standing near the edge. If no penguin is close enough to catch, the seal may try to drive the birds off the safety of the ice, then pursue them in an underwater chase.

One popular hunting method is for a seal to lie quietly in the water near shore facing out to sea, where it is hidden between pieces of floating ice. Returning penguins literally swim into the seal's jaws. The most common technique is for a leopard seal to patrol an ice edge where the penguins must leap up out of the water onto the ice in order to reach shore. When the tide is out, the ice edge may be five feet (1.5 m) high, and the birds may have to make many leaps before they succeed. The tired penguins are easy targets.

Penguins are not totally defenseless. To begin with, they are sharp-sighted, accomplished divers that are more at home underwater than any other seabird. This alone gives them a great advantage. Furthermore, they use a couple of other tricks to stack the odds in their favor.

Whenever penguins leave or return to a colony, they travel in groups—the bigger, the better. A group of penguins is more likely to spot an approaching seal, so there is less chance of a surprise attack. As well, an individual bird fleeing in a group is less likely to be singled out by a predator. Another way penguins outwit their enemies is by porpoising. As we've discussed, a porpoising penguin is more difficult for an underwater seal to track and follow, and many penguins swim this way whenever they are close to shore and predators are lurking.

More Hungry Mouths

On a warm, sunny afternoon one December, I watched the shoreline where the members of a mixed colony of gentoos and magellanic penguins were landing. I wrote in my journal: "I never saw the killer whales until they were very close to shore. There were four, maybe five animals in the pod, including a large adult male with a six-foot-tall [2 m] dorsal fin. The orcas were swimming slowly through a thick forest of giant kelp just offshore. Suddenly, one of the whales rushed forward, and ahead of it, half a dozen gentoo penguins porpoised to the surface as if they had been shot from a cannon. One of the whales spouted in a swirl of white water, then dove. When the penguins appeared next, they were spread out and porpoising rapidly toward shore. Moments later, individual birds began to pop safely out of the waves hitting the

At least one species of seal, fur seal or sea lion lives near every known penguin colony. On South Georgia, Antarctic fur seals lounge on the same beaches as king penguins, which they sometimes hunt and kill.

These Adélies are leaving their nesting colony on a feeding trip. They prefer to travel in large groups on such forays so that there are more sets of eyes to watch for leopard seals lurking near shore.

beach. The drama ended as fast as it began, and the whales disappeared around the point."

Killer whales probably hunt the larger species of penguins—the kings and emperors—more often than they do the smaller ones. The Crozet Islands, south of the Indian Ocean, are home to nearly 500,000 pairs of breeding king penguins, half of the world's population. French researchers have been studying the pods of orcas that live around these islands for many years, and they have frequently watched the black-and-white killers hunt and catch the kings. They have even seen a whale play with a live king as if it were a toy, tossing the bird into the air with its mouth, then leaping clear of the water and batting the penguin with a blow from its tail.

In warmer waters, barracuda and sharks also prey on penguins. In one colony of African penguins, for example, nearly half of the birds had lacerations on their feet and flippers. There are eight species of sharks in the offshore waters, but researchers believe the toothy culprit is likely the great white shark, the same predator known to attack human surfers off the beaches of California and Australia.

Young African penguins must sometimes deal with the most unexpected predator of all. In 1930, Cherry Kearton wrote this dramatic and colorful description: "The young [African] penguin meets his next enemies as soon as he goes to sea.... The penguin, floating probably and as yet barely able to swim, strays from the maternal care, out to the deeper water and close to rocks that overhang the most inviting pools. The octopus...with tentacles outstretched, [waits] for whatever may come within its reach. And then—a vicelike grip on dangling legs—a sudden pull, against which it is impossible to struggle—and one more penguin has disappeared."

CHAPTER 6

PARTING

PENGUINS

For most penguin chicks, family life comes to an end in January and February, the middle months of the southern summer. Typically, the family breaks up fairly quickly. Over the course of a week or two, first one parent stops its feeding visits, then the other. At this stage, the chicks are 2 to 4 months old, and many are nearly as big as their parents.

The young penguins no longer huddle in crèches; they either cluster in small groups at the edge of the colonies or hang out near the shoreline, watching the waves of adults come and go. Many of them are molting the last of the fluffy down they had as chicks, and they look quite comical. Tufts of down sprout from the tops of their heads like punk hairdos, and wispy strands still cling to their necks like the fur collar on a winter coat. Down feathers don't shed water the way the feathers of an adult do, and if a youngster wanders too close to the ocean and gets wet, the down hangs on its body in great soggy clumps, making it look even more comical.

It is at this age that curious young penguins begin to explore their world. Southern elephant seals share many beaches with penguins, and the seals haul out to molt at just about the time that penguin chicks are leaving home. A 14-foot (4 m) 9,000-pound (4,100 kg) bull elephant seal sprawled on the beach must be an irresistible temptation for a chick to investigate. On Macquarie Island, I watched a young king penguin nibble at the hind flipper of an elephant seal, then cry out in fright and flee as soon as the sluggish seal lifted its head and belched.

One adventurous chick even climbed on top of one of these monster beach slugs and, for a brief moment, was the lord of its universe. The seal arched up in annoyance, however, and the startled penguin tumbled off and hit the beach with its flippers and feet spinning in high gear.

Some of my best penguin experiences have been with young birds of this age. Often, I have sat quietly and let the youngsters waddle over and check me out. An experience I recorded in my field notes about a gang of young gentoos was fairly typical: "Within a few minutes, six or seven nearly full-grown chicks rocked their way over to investigate.

Young king penguin chicks such as this one are a curious lot. If you sit quietly on the ground, the youngsters often shuffle up to take a closer look and nibble on your sleeve or pants.

As they approached, they craned their necks in every conceivable direction, seemingly trying to figure out what kind of creature I was. After each bout of neck stretching, they shuffled ahead a few steps and repeated the inspection. If I moved suddenly, the penguins squawked in alarm, ran back a few steps, stopped and looked at me over their shoulders. In a few moments, their courage returned, and they eased toward me once more. Eventually, one bold chick, the largest in the group, tugged gently at the sleeve of my jacket. Satisfied that I was neither tasty nor dangerous, the daring chick turned away and waddled off. Clearly, there were more interesting discoveries to be made in life."

Chick Checkout

Early penguin researchers believed that chicks stayed ashore until starvation finally forced them into the ocean. Others thought that the parents lured their young into the water and taught them how to swim before the family broke up. Neither of these theories is accurate. In fact, there are no last-minute swimming lessons with a parent, and no adult bird feeds its offspring at sea. The young birds leave without their parents, although they may follow a group of adults. Many still have food in their stomachs, so it is unlikely that they have gone without eating for very long before they leave.

Over 2 months old, these rockhopper chicks are about to be left on their own by their parents. The young penguin in the center has molted most of its chick down and will soon have to learn to feed itself.

In crowded beach areas, some chicks are simply shoved into the water accidentally when a group of adults heads out to sea, or they are washed off the rocks by an unexpected wave.

No matter how or why a young penguin finally takes the plunge, once the chicks in a colony begin to leave, they all leave within a very short time. Researchers counted the chicks in an Adélie colony in the Ross Sea of Antarctica. On January 27, all the chicks in the colony were still ashore, loafing along the shoreline. Within three days, the first chicks began to leave, and after a week, half of them were gone. Within two weeks, every chick had left. At some large colonies, 50,000 chicks may leave within a one-week period. Chicks are clumsy swimmers and unaware of the danger from killer whales, sea lions and leopard seals. When so many young penguins leave at the same time, the local predators are flooded with more easy prey than they can hunt. As a result, even though the predators capture many chicks, many more escape and make it to the open sea.

When the young penguins reach the sea, there are no more free lunches. They must feed themselves for the first time. And if they thought their parents made them run for lunch in the colony, wait until they see how fast krill, fish and squid can move. Two events make a chick's first trip to sea a little easier to manage. First, the timing of chick departure often coincides with the peak of food production in the oceans where penguins live. The days are the longest of the year, plankton growth is at its maximum, and food is abundant, so even inexperienced penguin chicks can usually catch enough to eat. The timing also coincides with the annual molting period, when most of the adult birds in the colony are forced to stay on shore for up to a month or more. So for at least a few weeks, the chicks do not have to compete with experienced adults for food. By the time the adults return to the sea, the chicks are better at finding and catching their meals and better able to compete.

Fat for Feathers

Every activity in a penguin's life takes energy, and the three most expensive activities are reproduction, migration and molting. For penguins, molting is by far the most costly of the three. At the end of the breeding season, the adults go out to sea to feast and fatten. Sometimes it may take three weeks to plumpen up, sometimes three months. When they finally

An adult king penguin spends four to five weeks ashore each year shedding its old feathers and replacing them with new ones. During the process, it cannot go to sea to feed and so may lose up to half of its body weight.

return to shore, they are the fattest they will be at any time of the year. Some may be so padded that they can barely climb up the beach to reach a resting spot. The majority of penguins return to their breeding colonies to molt. The two most polar species, Adélies and emperors, usually stay on the sea ice or hop aboard an iceberg and float while they molt.

Most penguin species spend two to four weeks replacing their feathers, but in the large kings and emperors, it may require four to six weeks. A penguin fasts for the entire molting period and may lose half of its body weight. Other species of birds, such as ducks and geese, may become flightless when they molt, but none lose all their feathers at once, and none are forced to stay out of water, as are penguins. There are a couple of good reasons why the molting pattern in penguins is so different from that of other birds. To begin with, if a penguin goes into the water while it is molting, it can lose excessive amounts of body heat and its temperature may drop. When researchers immersed a molting Galápagos penguin in water at 70 degrees F (21°C), the bird's body temperature dropped 10 Fahrenheit degrees (5.5C°) in just 30 seconds.

Another reason for a molting penguin to stay on shore is that the frayed plumage of a molting penguin destroys the bird's streamlined profile, slowing it down and making it more vulnerable

This yearling magellanic penguin has come ashore in early December to molt. Without the responsibilities of raising a family, juvenile penguins molt several months earlier than the adults.

to predators. As well, a slower penguin might burn up more energy when hunting than it gains by eating what it catches.

The molting phase for most penguin species is the final event in the breeding season. After this, more than half of the species migrate to sea and disappear for six months or so, until they return once again the following spring to their crowded colonies—the "ancient grave-yards" of their ancestors.

In the 1970s, conservationists were worried about the survival of only three penguin species: African, Humboldt and Galápagos. In the 1980s, their concerns grew, when seven species of penguins were in trouble. In 1996, an international meeting of penguin experts agreed that nine penguin species were either vulnerable or endangered. Penguins are in trouble for many reasons: overfishing, loss of nesting habitats, oil pollution, global warming and uncontrolled tourism and disturbance of their breeding grounds. This remarkable family of birds has been on Earth since the Age of Dinosaurs. My only hope for their future is perhaps best expressed by the words of veteran penguin researcher Dr. Bernard Stonehouse, who wrote: "I have had the impression that to penguins, man is just another penguin—different, less predictable, occasionally violent, but tolerable company when he sits still and minds his own business."

King penguins have the longest chick-rearing period of any bird. It takes 12 to 14 months from the time the young penguins hatch to the time they start to molt their fuzzy coats of down.

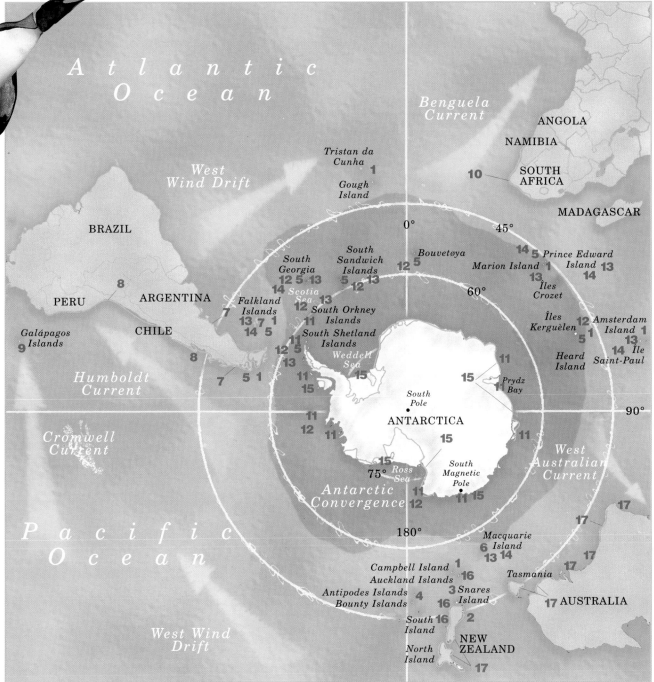

Atlantic Ocean

Benguela Current

ANGOLA

NAMIBIA

SOUTH AFRICA

10

MADAGASCAR

West Wind Drift

Tristan da Cunha
1

Gough Island

0°   45°

BRAZIL

South Georgia
12 5 13
14

South Sandwich Islands
5 13

Scotia Sea
12

Bouvetøya
5

12

14 5 *Prince Edward Island* 13
1 14

Marion Island 13

60°

Îles Crozet 13

PERU

ARGENTINA

Falkland Islands
13 7 1
14 5

CHILE

South Orkney Islands
11

South Shetland Islands
12 11
13

Weddell Sea
15

Îles Kerguèlen
5

12 *Amsterdam Island* 1
1

13

14 *Île Saint-Paul*

Galápagos Islands
9

Heard Island

8

7 5 1

8

11
15

11

15

15 *Prydz Bay*
11

Humboldt Current

South Pole

ANTARCTICA

90°

11

Cromwell Current

11
12

11

15

11

West Australian Current

75° *Ross Sea*

15

South Magnetic Pole

15

Pacific Ocean

Antarctic Convergence

11
12

11 15

180°

Macquarie Island
6
13 14

17

Campbell Island 1
Auckland Islands 16

Tasmania

17

17

Antipodes Islands
Bounty Islands
16

4

3 *Snares Island*

17 AUSTRALIA

South Island 16

2

West Wind Drift

North Island

NEW ZEALAND

17

1 Rockhopper
(*Eudyptes chrysocome*)

2 Fiordland
(*Eudyptes pachyrhynchus*)

3 Snares
(*Eudyptes robustus*)

4 Erect-crested
(*Eudyptes sclateri*)

5 Macaroni
(*Eudyptes chrysolophus*)

6 Royal
(*Eudyptes schlegeli*)

7 Magellanic
(*Spheniscus magellanicus*)

8 Humboldt
(*Spheniscus humboldti*)

9 Galápagos
(*Spheniscus mendiculus*)

10 African or Jackass
(*Spheniscus demersus*)

11 Adélie
(*Pygoscelis adeliae*)

12 Chinstrap
(*Pygoscelis antarctica*)

13 Gentoo
(*Pygoscelis papua*)

14 King
(*Aptenodytes patagonicus*)

15 Emperor
(*Aptenodytes forsteri*)

16 Yellow-eyed
(*Megadyptes antipodes*)

17 Little or Fairy
(*Eudyptula minor*)

In 1979, at the age of 31, Dr. Wayne Lynch left a career in emergency medicine to work full-time as a science writer and photographer. Today, he is Canada's best-known and most widely published professional wildlife photographer. His photo credits include hundreds of magazine covers, thousands of calendar shots and tens of thousands of images published in over 30 countries. He is also the author and photographer of a dozen highly acclaimed natural-history books, including *Wild Birds Across the Prairies*; *Penguins of the World*; *Bears, Bears, Bears*; *A is for Arctic: Natural Wonders of a Polar World*; and *Married to the Wind: A Study of the Prairie Grasslands*. His books have been described as "a magical combination of words and images."

Dr. Lynch has studied wildlife in over 60 countries and is a Fellow of the internationally recognized Explorers Club, headquartered in New York City. A Fellow is someone who has actively participated in exploration or has substantially enlarged the scope of human knowledge through scientific achievements and published reports, books and articles. In 1997, Dr. Lynch was elected as a Fellow to the Arctic Institute of North America, in recognition of his contributions to the knowledge of polar and subpolar regions. He is seen here with some of his many Adélie friends.